World History Quick Starts

Author: Wendi Silvano
Editor: Mary Dieterich
Proofreaders: April Albert and Margaret Brown

COPYRIGHT © 2020 Mark Twain Media, Inc.

ISBN 978-1-62223-828-6

Printing No. CD-405060

Mark Twain Media, Inc., Publishers
Distributed by Carson-Dellosa Publishing LLC

The purchase of this book entitles the buyer to reproduce the student pages for classroom use only. Other permissions may be obtained by writing Mark Twain Media, Inc., Publishers.

All rights reserved. Printed in the United States of America.

Table of Contents

Introduction to the Teacher

It is important for students to periodically review the information they have previously learned. *World History Quick Starts* helps students do just that while also preparing them for the day's lesson by focusing on the topic of ancient world civilizations.

The short quick start activities in this book provide opportunities for students to review what they have learned. Each page contains two to four quick starts. The topics cover a range of world civilizations from the eastern and western hemispheres.

Suggestions for using warm-up activities:

- Copy and cut apart one or more pages each week. Give students one quick start each day at the beginning of class.

- Give each student a copy of the entire page to keep in their binders to complete as assigned.

- Make transparencies of individual quick starts and complete activities as a group.

- Put copies of quick starts in a learning center for individual students to complete on their own when they have a few extra minutes.

- Use quick starts as homework assignments.

- Use quick starts as questions in a review game.

- Keep some quick starts on hand to use when the class has a few extra minutes before dismissal.

Prehistory

Prehistory 1

Match each term with its definition.

1. A scientist who examines objects to learn about past cultures. _Archaeologist_

2. A person who studies the written and oral records of human cultures. _historian_

3. Stories passed down by word of mouth. _oral traditions_

4. The period of time from the past before writing was invented. _prehistory_

5. Things shaped by humans, such as tools, pottery, and weapons. _Artifacts_

6. Evidence of plant or animal life preserved in stone. _fossils_

prehistory
oral traditions
fossils
archaeologist
artifacts
historian

Prehistory 2

Explain at least two ways in which geography affects a civilization.

_____

_____

_____

_____

_____

_____

_____

_____

Prehistory

Prehistory 3

Write a definition for each of these terms.

1. nomad _____
   _____
2. fertile _____
   _____
3. irrigation _____
   _____
4. civilization _____
   _____

Prehistory 4

Circle the Stone Age characteristic from each pair.

1. People used simple stone tools.   People used tools made of bronze.

2. Many civilizations began.   People were primarily nomads.

3. Homes were made of adobe.   People lived in caves or camped.

4. Governments developed.   Each family or group ruled itself.

Prehistory 5

Unscramble the names of some of the things artisans made in pre-historical times.

1. K T B S A E S _____
2. H A L R E E T   D O S G O _____
3. L O S O T _____
4. T R Y O T E P _____
5. T G O I H N C L _____
6. S C I M U L A   R M T N I E N S T U S _____

Early Middle Eastern Civilizations

Fertile Crescent & Mesopotamia 1

List two reasons why the Fertile Crescent was an ideal place for nomadic people to settle and build cities.

1. _____

   _____

   _____

2. _____

   _____

   _____

Fertile Crescent & Mesopotamia 2

Unscramble the names of these modern countries that exist in the areas in and around the Fertile Crescent.

1. L S E I R A _____
2. B N O E A N L _____
3. R A Y S I _____
4. Q R I A _____
5. R N A I _____
6. U A S I D B R I A A A

   _____

Fertile Crescent & Mesopotamia 3

1. The Greek word *Mesopotamia* means "between two rivers." Name the two rivers that surrounded Mesopotamia.

   _____

   _____

2. Name two modern-day countries these rivers cross before they empty into the Persian Gulf.

   _____

   _____

Fertile Crescent & Mesopotamia 4

Fill in the blanks.

> language
> city-states
> civilization
> cultures
> government

Mesopotamia was not a _____, but rather an area. It was composed of several _____, each having its own religion, laws, _____, and _____.

Sometimes different _____ existed at the same time in the area.

Early Middle Eastern Civilizations

Fertile Crescent & Mesopotamia 5

Put a check mark by each sentence about the Fertile Crescent that is correct.

1. ____ People living in the Fertile Crescent began to trade because they could grow more crops and raise more animals than they needed.
2. ____ Trading led to population decreases.
3. ____ Increased population led to the need to develop laws.
4. ____ Many different civilizations developed in the Fertile Crescent.

The Sumerians 1

Circle the inventions that were developed by the Sumerians.

written language

wheel

water clock

sailboat

iron nails

plow

twelve-month calendar

loom

The Sumerians 2

Write *T* for true or *F* for false.

1. ____ Sumerian architecture had archways for doors and gates.
2. ____ Sumerians made temples called ziggurats.
3. ____ Sumerians believed in only one god.
4. ____ Sumerians believed the priests were representatives of gods.

The Sumerians 3

One major problem for Sumer was the lack of natural protection for Mesopotamia. Why was that a disadvantage? Write your opinion on your own paper.

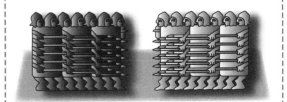

Early Middle Eastern Civilizations

The Sumerians 4

Write a definition for each of the terms.

1. pictographs _____
   _____

2. scribes _____
   _____

3. stylus _____
   _____

4. cuneiform _____
   _____

The Sumerians 5

Change the underlined words to make the information correct.

The Sumerians were the first group of people to inhabit

Greece. They controlled the Tigris and the Nile Rivers by building levees and

used flooding to water the outlying areas of land. They built temples called

pyramids and believed in many gods. They developed a numbering system

based on the number fifty, which we still use today for measuring distance.

Babylonia 1

By each statement, write *Wall* if it applies to the Wall of Babylon, write *Gate* for the Gate of Ishtar, or write *Gardens* for the Hanging Gardens of Babylon.

1. had four towers from which guards could watch _____
2. named after a goddess _____
3. built to please Nebuchadnezzar's wife _____
4. had terraces covered in plants and pools _____
5. wide enough that a four-horse chariot could drive on it _____
6. made of colorful, glazed bricks with pictures of animals _____

Early Middle Eastern Civilizations

Babylonia 2

Write *Yes* or *No* to show if each sentence is true.

1. ＿＿ The Babylonians adopted much of the Sumerian culture.
2. ＿＿ Akkad was a king of Babylonia.
3. ＿＿ Babylon expanded by conquering other kingdoms.
4. ＿＿ Babylonians knew little of astronomy.

Babylonia 3

According to the Code of Hammurabi, which statement in each pair is true? Circle your choice.

1. Protected the weak
   Favored the ruling class only

2. Read only by priests
   Carved on a stone column for all to see

3. Eye-for-eye punishments
   Punished only the highest offenses

4. Applied to women and slaves
   Applied only to men and masters

Babylonia 4

Fill in the blanks with the correct word.

Babylonian astronomy was advanced for its time. Babylonians kept records of events such as

e ＿ ＿ ＿ ＿ ＿ ＿ ＿ and

measured time by studying the

m ＿ ＿ ＿ ＿ ＿ ＿ ＿ of the

celestial bodies. Babylonian priests even claimed they could predict the

f ＿ ＿ ＿ ＿ ＿ by studying the

stars and p ＿ ＿ ＿ ＿ ＿ ＿ ＿.

Babylonia 5

List three interesting facts about Babylonia.

1. ＿＿＿＿＿＿＿＿＿＿＿＿
   ＿＿＿＿＿＿＿＿＿＿＿＿
   ＿＿＿＿＿＿＿＿＿＿＿＿

2. ＿＿＿＿＿＿＿＿＿＿＿＿
   ＿＿＿＿＿＿＿＿＿＿＿＿
   ＿＿＿＿＿＿＿＿＿＿＿＿

3. ＿＿＿＿＿＿＿＿＿＿＿＿
   ＿＿＿＿＿＿＿＿＿＿＿＿
   ＿＿＿＿＿＿＿＿＿＿＿＿

Early Middle Eastern Civilizations

The Assyrians 1

Write *T* for true or *F* for false.

1. ____ The Assyrian kingdom was on the upper Tigris River.
2. ____ Assyrian land was watered by rain and by the Tigris River.
3. ____ Assyria was protected from attacks by Barbarians.
4. ____ The original capital of Assyria was Ashur.

The Assyrians 2

Assyria's army was a "standing army," rather than a "citizen-soldier" army. Explain what the difference is.

_____

_____

_____

_____

_____

_____

_____

_____

The Assyrians 3

Circle the statement that was not an Assyrian achievement. On your own paper, pick one Assyrian achievement and explain it in more detail.

1. Developed a library
2. Made a written language
3. Built a system of roads
4. Developed mail service

The Assyrians 4

Assyria's army was highly disciplined and greatly feared. Put a check by the items below that the Assyrian army used.

____ cannons

____ chariots

____ muskets

____ cavalry

____ archers

____ foot soldiers

____ weapons made of iron

____ iron-tipped battering rams

Early Middle Eastern Civilizations

The Assyrians 5

Fill in the blanks.

mercenaries	governor
soldiers	king fort

Once Assyrians conquered a city, they built a _____ and

appointed a _____ to rule the city. He reported directly to the

_____. There were not enough _____ to support

all these forts, so Assyrians hired _____ from other countries.

The Hittites 1

The Hittites signed the first recorded peace treaty in history.

PEACE

1. With whom did the Hittites sign a treaty?

   _____

2. What did these two kingdoms promise to do for each other?

   _____

   _____

   _____

The Hittites 2

Write *T* for true or *F* for false.

____ 1. Hattusa was the Hittites' capital city.

____ 2. Knowledge of steel metallurgy began
     with the Hittites.

____ 3. The Hittites used one main language.

____ 4. Hittite law compensated people who were wronged.

____ 5. The Hittite Empire was between the Tigris and the Euphrates Rivers.

Early Middle Eastern Civilizations

The Hittites 3

Fill in the blanks.

The Hittites were originally migrant

_____, who moved into

_____. They were not as

organized as other _____, with

city-states that were quite spread out. Each city-state maintained

its own language and _____. They often

fought amongst themselves until _____ became king.

Then the empire grew to include most of modern-day _____.

> civilizations
> Turkey
> peasants
> Anatolia
> religion
> Labarnas

The Hittites 4

Match each date to the correct statement.

> a. 1000   b. 26
> c. 1595   d. 1200

1. The Hittite culture lasted from 1750 B.C. to _____ B.C.

2. The capital city, Hattusa, had a stone wall _____ feet thick.

3. The Hittites worshipped about _____ gods.

4. The Hittities sacked Babylonia in the year _____ B.C.

The Hittites 5

Circle all the phrases that refer to the Hittites.

1. Signed a treaty

2. Had one distinct culture

3. Developed the process of smelting

4. Were warlike

5. Introduced horses to the Middle East

6. Had laws considered cruel

Early Middle Eastern Civilizations

The Phoenicians 1

Write *T* for true or *F* for false.

_____ 1. Phoenicians lived on the Egyptian coast.

_____ 2. Phoenicians were the greatest traders of the ancient world.

_____ 3. Phoenicians improved glass making.

_____ 4. Their greatest achievement was the alphabet.

The Phoenicians 2

Fill in the blanks.

expensive	Tyre
royalty	dye
Sidon	purple

The two main Phoenician cities were _____ and _____. Phoenicians developed a process of making purple _____. The Greek word *phoinix* means _____, so the Phoenicians were Purple Men. The dye was _____, so it was mainly used by _____.

The Phoenicians 3

1. How was the Phoenician alphabet different from writings such as cuneiform?

_____

_____

2. How many symbols did it include?

_____

3. What did each symbol represent?

_____

The Phoenicians 4

Fill in the missing vowels from these items that the Phoenicians traded.

1. c __ l __ r __ d
   gl __ ssw __ r __
2. __ v __ ry and w __ __ d
   c __ rv __ ngs
3. __ mbr __ __ d __ r __ d
   cl __ th
4. p __ tt __ ry
5. w __ n __

Early Middle Eastern Civilizations

The Phoenicians 5

Change the underlined word to make each sentence true.

1. The Phoenicians' skill in <u>building</u> developed as they searched for new trading markets.
2. The Phoenicians developed a process of making <u>red</u> dye.
3. Phoenicians sailed all over the <u>Black</u> Sea to trade.
4. The Phoenician alphabet's symbols each represented a <u>thing</u>.

The Hebrews 1

The Hebrews were one of the first groups to practice monotheism instead of polytheism. Explain what the difference is.

_____

_____

_____

_____

_____

_____

_____

_____

The Hebrews 2

Unscramble the names of these Hebrew leaders.

1. B H A R A M A

   _____

2. S O M S E

   _____

3. V D I A D

   _____

4. U S L A

   _____

5. L M O N O S O

   _____

The Hebrews 3

What am I?

_____

Clue one:　I am a set of laws based on the Hebrew religion.

Clue two:　I am found in the Old Testament in the Bible.

Clue three:　The Hebrews believed these laws were from God.

Early Middle Eastern Civilizations

The Hebrews 4

Fill in the blanks.

> Canaan   enslaved   pharaoh
> Abraham   famine   Egypt

_____ led the Hebrews into _____.

A _____ in the land caused them to flee to

_____. There they lived and flourished for 600 years,

but were later _____ by the Egyptian

_____, who was jealous of their wealth.

The Hebrews 5

Three major religions developed in the Hebrew capital of Jerusalem. What are they?

1. _____

2. _____

3 _____

The Persians 1

Place a check by the facts that are correct.

1. ___ Cyrus and his army conquered most of the ancient world.

2. ___ Persians treated those they conquered with cruelty.

3. ___ Persians allowed the conquered to keep their cultures.

4. ___ Those conquered by Persia paid taxes to Cyrus.

5. ___ Cyrus enslaved the Jews.

Early Middle Eastern Civilizations

The Persians 2

Fill in the blanks.

| Zoroaster |
| Avesta |
| Ahura Mazda |
| Ahriman |

1. _____ is the Persians' sacred book.

2. _____ is the founder of the Persian religion, Zoroastrianism.

3. _____ is the god of goodness, wisdom, and truth to the Persians.

4. _____ is the evil spirit.

The Persians 3

Rewrite the following paragraph on your own paper to make the underlined words correct.

After Cyrus died, his son-in-law, <u>Alexander</u>, continued his rule. He divided the empire into <u>12</u> provinces called <u>Avestas</u>. Each was ruled by a governor called a <u>sultan</u>. The Persians improved an extensive <u>water</u> system to help with transportation and communication. This encouraged international <u>fears</u>, as people were able to carry their wares more easily.

The Persians 4

Label the following items on the Persian Empire map.

A. The Mediterranean Sea
B. The Tigris River
C. The Black Sea
D. The Euphrates River
E. The Caspian Sea
F. The Nile River
G. The Red Sea
H. The Persian Gulf

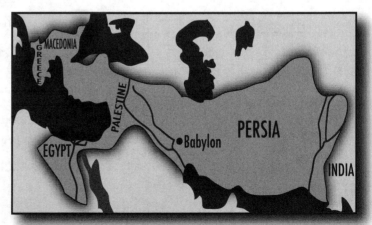

Ancient Egypt

Ancient Egypt 1

Change the underlined words to make the information correct.

The annual flooding of the <u>Amazon</u> River in Egypt leaves behind a layer of rich <u>grass</u>, perfect for growing crops. People were drawn to the area because of the soil. It became the home of one of the world's <u>latest</u> civilizations — the Egyptians. It was the longest-lasting civilization in history, lasting over <u>1,000</u> years. The Egyptians called the fertile strip the "<u>Yellow</u> Land," because of the soil, and the surrounding <u>mountains</u> the "Red Land."

Ancient Egypt 2

Write these Egyptian numbers in our number system.

1	I	10	∩
2	II	20	∩∩
3	III	30	∩∩∩
4	IIII	40	∩∩ ∩∩
5	III II	100	℮
6	III III	1000	𓆼
7	IIII III	10,000	𓂭
8	IIII IIII	100,000	𓆐
9	III III III	1,000,000	𓁨

1. ℮℮℮ ∩∩∩ IIII = _____
   ℮℮℮ ∩∩∩∩

2. 𓀀𓀀 ℮ ∩∩∩∩ III = _____

3. 𓆼 𓀀𓀀 ℮ ∩∩ III II = _____

4. ℮℮℮ ∩∩ III IIII = _____

Ancient Egypt 3

Match the pharaohs.

    a. Tutankhamen   b. Ramses II   c. Hatshepsut
    d. Thutmose III   e. Menes

1. ____ Female ruler – time of peace and prosperity
2. ____ Began first dynasty – united Upper and Lower Egypt
3. ____ Became pharaoh at 8 years of age
4. ____ Brilliant military leader, conquered Palestine and Syria
5. ____ Reigned for 67 years – fought the Hittites

Ancient Egypt

Ancient Egypt 4

Unscramble the names of these structures the ancient Egyptians built.

1. H X S N P I

   _____

2. S M R Y P A I D

   _____

3. N L A S C A

   _____

4. M P S E L T E

   _____

Ancient Egypt 5

What is it?

1. A reed-like plant used to make a paper-like material: _____

2. The Egyptian king or ruler:

   _____

3. A large stone tomb built for a pharaoh: _____

4. Dried and wrapped bodies:

   _____

5. A system of writing using pictures: _____

Ancient Egypt 6

Name three things the Egyptians brought back from Nubia.

1. _____

2. _____

3 _____

Ancient Egypt 7

Write the letter of the correct kingdom beside each item to indicate when the item happened.

   a. Old   b. Middle   c. New

____ 1. Tutankhamen

____ 2. Menes

____ 3. Mentuhotep

____ 4. Akhetaton

____ 5. Thebes

____ 6. Memphis

____ 7. Aton worshipped

____ 8. pyramids built

Ancient Egypt

Ancient Egypt 8

Circle the words related to Ancient Egypt.

cuneiform   pyramids

Nile   hieroglyphics

mercenaries   pharaoh

nomarchs   Khufu

gunpowder   papyrus

Ashur   scribes

Aton   mummies

Thebes   democracy

Ancient Egypt 9

Put a check by those facts that are correct.

1. ___ Most Egyptians could read and write.
2. ___ Scribes were priests and administrators.
3. ___ Pharaohs were considered gods.
4. ___ Most mummies were placed inside a sarcophagus.
5. ___ Egyptians wore snake charms.

Ancient Egypt 10

Explain how the geography of the land in Egypt served as a natural barrier to protect the Egyptians. Use your own paper.

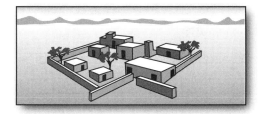

Ancient Egypt 11

Write *T* for true or *F* for false.

1. ___ Egyptians believed in an afterlife.
2. ___ Egyptians worshipped many gods.
3. ___ Egyptians were buried wearing amulets as punishment for wrongs they committed in life.
4. ___ Egyptians were excellent craftsmen, scholars, and engineers.

Ancient Egypt

Ancient Egypt 12

Write *T* for true or *F* for false.

1. ____ The Nile flows into the Black Sea.
2. ____ The Nile is the world's longest river.
3. ____ The Nile is more than 4,000 miles (6,400 km) long.
4. ____ The Nile's two main sources are the Blue Nile and the Red Nile.
5. ____ The Nile flows from south to north.

Ancient Egypt 13

Circle the things that are true about Egyptian pharaohs.

1. They had absolute power.
2. They were the creators of the world.
3. They owned all land and water.
4. They were buried at sea.
5. They were religious leaders.
6. They were believed to be gods.
7. They were always male.

Ancient Egypt 14

Number these steps in order of the process of mummification.

a. ____ The body was cleaned and bathed in spices.
b. ____ The body was wrapped with long linen bandages.
c. ____ The organs were removed from the body.
d. ____ The wrapped body was placed inside a sarcophagus.
e. ____ The body was filled with salt and stored to dry out.

Ancient Egypt 15

Fill in the blanks.

> Bow   tradesmen   gold   Nubia

For many years, _____ and Egypt were friendly neighbors. The Egyptians called Nubia "The Land of the _____," because of the great skill of Nubian archers. Egyptian _____ brought many goods from Lower Nubia, including _____.

Ancient Egypt

Ancient Egypt 16

Using your own paper, explain the significance of the
Rosetta Stone and Jean-François Champollion.

_____

_____

_____

_____

_____

Ancient Egypt 17

Write *Yes* or *No* to indicate if each statement is true.

1. _____ Egyptian writing was called cuneiform.

2. _____ Many Egyptian writings are on papyrus scrolls.

3. _____ Egyptians invented a calendar with 365 days.

4. _____ Egyptians used surgery and herbs to cure illness.

5. _____ The Egyptians used a loom to weave cloth.

Ancient Egypt 18

Circle the statement from each pair that is true about
Egyptian women.

1. They had many different occupations.
   They were almost all homemakers.

2. They could not own property.   They could own property.

3. Some were in charge of temples.   They could not work at religious sites.

4. They worked in the fields with men. They did not work in the fields.

The Indus Valley & Ancient India

Indus Valley 1

Circle the phrases that describe the Indus Valley civilization.

1. undeciphered language
2. larger cities than Sumeria
3. drainage and sewer system
4. uncovered in 1921
5. many wars
6. well-planned cities
7. in China
8. narrow streets
9. grew cotton

Indus Valley 2

List two interesting facts about the people of the Indus Valley.

1. _____

   _____

   _____

   _____

2. _____

   _____

   _____

   _____

Indus Valley 3

Unscramble the names of the crops and animals raised in the Indus Valley.

1. L A R E B Y   _____
2. A T E W H   _____
3. T A E S D   _____
4. A T L E C T   _____
5. K H I C E C S N _____
6. U F A B F O L   _____

Indus Valley 4

Why did so many of the early civilizations, such as the Indus Valley civilization, spring up along the banks of large rivers? Write your opinion on your own paper.

The Indus Valley & Ancient India

Indus Valley 5

Fill in the blanks.

cotton   Ganges   Harappa
Indus   Pakistan   Mohenjo-daro

The Indus Valley was located in the western part of what is now

_____, on the banks of the _____

River and the upper _____ River. The two large cities,

_____ and _____, were full of

craftsmen and merchants. The people of this valley were one of the first groups

to grow _____ and domesticate animals.

Ancient India 1

Fill in the blanks.

Alexander   Babylon   artists
thousand   Sanskrit   ideas

_____ the Great conquered Ancient India in 325 B.C.

He then returned to _____. He left behind several

_____ Greek soldiers, teachers, and _____.

The Greeks and Indians exchanged many _____. The

period after Alexander's departure saw a great production of Indian literature

written in _____, including the *Reg Veda* and the

Ramayana.

Ancient India 2

Write *Yes* or *No* to indicate if each statement is true.

1. _____ Indians invented steel after learning how to make
   iron from the Assyrians.

2. _____ The most important Indian Hindu text is the *Bhagavad Gita*.

3. _____ When Indians rediscovered writing, they developed Sanskrit.

4. _____ Millions of Indians converted to Buddhism around 2000 B.C.

5. _____ Indians invented numerical zero around 600 A.D.

The Indus Valley & Ancient India

Ancient India 3

Fill in the blanks.

| spirit | gods | | beliefs |
| many | goddesses | | |

      Hinduism absorbed many _____ from other religions. Hindus believe there are _____ ways to worship. There is no one single _____ of the Hindu religion. They worship many _____ and _____. The *Bhagavad Gita* is the poem that sums up the main ideas of the Hindu faith. After becoming Buddhist, many ancient Indians later went back to Hinduism but kept Buddha as a god.

Ancient India 4

Answer the following questions on your own paper.

    Hindus believe in reincarnation, or the idea that when you die your soul is reborn in the body of another living thing.

1. What determined in what type of body you would be reborn?
2. What form might you take if you acted badly in life?
3. What would happen if you lived a perfect life?

Ancient India 5

Write *Yes* or *No* to indicate if these items are a Buddhist belief.

1. _____ The answer to human suffering is right thinking and self-denial.
2. _____ People should be unselfish and treat others fairly.
3. _____ Priests are those endowed with special powers.
4. _____ "Nirvana" is a state of lasting peace.
5. _____ People should avoid violence and not kill any living thing.

The Far East

Ancient China 1

Write *T* for true or *F* for false.

1. ____ Southern China is wet and warm because of monsoons.

2. ____ Ancient Chinese were isolated from other ancient civilizations.

3. ____ The northern part of China is very dry.

4. ____ China borders the Atlantic Ocean.

Ancient China 2

Fill in the blanks.

> farming   Yellow   soil
> muddiest   plains

The Huang He river is the

_____ river in the world.

It is often called the _____

River because of the yellow-brown

_____ the water carries.

When the Huang He floods, it carpets the

surrounding _____

with soil, which is good for

_____.

Ancient China 3

Why was the Huang He River called "China's Sorrow"?

_____

_____

_____

_____

_____

_____

_____

_____

Ancient China 4

The Shang dynasty was the first known Chinese civilization. On your own paper, rewrite these sentences about the Shang dynasty so they make sense.

1. built cities Shang The people the first China in

2. workers finest the bronze in Shang The China people were of some

3. invented writing Shang The China's first people

The Far East

Ancient China 5

Circle the statement from each pair that is true concerning Chinese families.

1. Many generations lived together.   Each generation lived separately.

2. The oldest male had top authority.   The strongest male had top authority.

3. Chinese youth chose their own spouses.   Parents chose spouses.

4. Chinese family names are first.   Chinese family names are last.

Ancient China 6

Fill in the blanks.

dynasty	Qin	harsh
Great Wall	united	

Shi Huangdi was the ruler who _____ China. He ruled the _____ people who lived along China's western edge. His _____ is named after the Qin people. He was a _____ ruler who wanted to change China. He ordered the construction of the _____ of China.

Ancient China 7

Fill in the blanks.

Antioch	ideas	Han
stable	Silk	

The _____ dynasty brought a more _____ government to China. This dynasty lasted for about 400 years. During this dynasty, traders traveled a route to _____ that was called the _____ Road. This was a very dangerous route, but it brought both new goods and _____ to China.

The Far East

Ancient China 8

Who am I?

_____

Clue one: I am considered early China's greatest thinker.

Clue two: I tried to pass on forgotten teachings about peace, stability, and prosperity.

Clue three: The Chinese version of my name is Kong Fu Zi or "Master Kong."

Ancient China 9

Circle the inventions credited to the Chinese.

papyrus   silk   rockets

sewers   chess   book printing

keystones   kites   gunpowder

fireworks   paper   wheelbarrows

matches   abacus   porcelain

Ancient China 10

Lao-tzu was another great Chinese teacher with a philosophy different from that of Confucius. Write *C* for Confucius or *L* for Lao-tzu next to each belief to indicate who taught it.

1. ____ withdraw from society
2. ____ politeness, sincerity, unselfishness, hard work
3. ____ work to improve society
4. ____ live simple lives in harmony with nature
5. ____ show respect to those above and below them

Ancient China 11

What am I?

_____

Clue one: I am a small insect.

Clue two: I feed on mulberry leaves.

Clue three: I produce something that was spun into a precious fabric in China.

The Far East

Ancient China 12

What do you consider to be the greatest invention of the Chinese? Why?

_____

_____

_____

_____

_____

Ancient China 13

Circle the sentences about the Great Wall of China that are true.

1.   The Great Wall of China was built all at the same time.

2.   The Great Wall of China is two walls filled with dirt and lined with stone.

3.   The Wall as we know it today was built during the Ming dynasty.

4.   The Great Wall of China was built as a decoration.

5.   Parts of the Great Wall of China have been taken down.

Ancient China 14

How do you think the stability of the Han dynasty is related to the numerous accomplishments and inventions that occurred during that time?

_____

_____

_____

_____

_____

The Far East

Ancient China 15

Fill in the missing vowels to complete the names of these Chinese dynasties.

1. S h __ n g   2. C h __ __

3. M __ n c h __   4. M __ n g

5. T __ n g   6. S __ __

7. Q __ n   8. Z h __ __

9. H __ n   10. X __ __

11. S __ n g

The Mongols 1

Who am I?

_____

Clue one: My name means "mighty lord."

Clue two: I was one of the greatest conquerors of all time.

Clue three: I led the Mongols in an invasion of China in 1211.

The Mongols 2

Fill in the blanks.

> Europe   brutal   largest   feared
> animals   Asia   destroyed

The Mongol Empire became the _____, most

powerful, and most _____ empire the world has ever

known. The Mongols were so fast they could outrun _____.

They were _____ as soldiers. They often

_____ everything and everyone in

their path. The Mongol Empire eventually encompassed

most of _____ and parts of _____.

The Far East

The Mongols 3

The Mongols lived on land called a "steppe." Check the sentences that are correct about this region.

1. ___ The steppe is a high grassland.
2. ___ The steppe is similar to the pampas in South America.
3. ___ Temperatures are mild in the steppe.
4. ___ "Steppe" is a Slavic word.

The Mongols 4

Unscramble the underlined words.

1. Every Mongol man was a d l o s r i e. _____
2. To the Chinese, the Mongols were b r n s r a b a i a. _____
3. The Mongols had well-trained r s h o e s. _____
4. The Mongols mastered the use of Chinese e s w a p n o. _____

The Mongols 5

Fill in the blanks.

Beijing	revolted	ruled	erase	Ming

The Chinese finally _____ against the Mongol rulers and drove them out. The rebel leader, named Ming Hong Wu, founded the _____ dynasty that _____ China. They tried to _____ all traces of the Mongols. The Mongol city of _____ became the imperial capital.

The Greek World

The Minoans 1

Write *T* for true or *F* for false.

1. ___ The Minoan civilization was the first civilization in Europe.

2. ___ The Minoan civilization existed mostly on the island of Crete.

3. ___ Minoan women were treated poorly.

4. ___ The Minoans had more social equality than other early civilizations.

5. ___ Minoans had more leisure time than other early civilizations.

The Minoans 2

Fill in the blanks.

somersault
boxing
horns
bull-jumping
sports
feet

Because of their wealth, Minoans had time for
_____. Two examples were
_____ and _____.

In bull-jumping, a bull is released to charge a jumper. He or she must grab the
bull by the _____ and jump onto its back or leap over the bull,
turn a _____ in the air, and land gracefully on his or her
_____.

The Minoans 3

Circle the statement from each pair that is true concerning Minoan life.

1. All Minoans had comfortable homes.   Poor Minoans lived in shacks.

2. Minoan homes were all one story.   Most Minoan homes were two stories.

3. Almost all Minoans were farmers.   Many Minoans were craftsmen.

4. Each Minoan town had a palace.   Only the Minoan capital had a palace.

The Greek World

The Minoans 4

What was the advantage for the Minoan Civilization of being on an island? What effects did it have on the economy and the lifestyle of the Minoans? Write a response on your own paper.

The Minoans 5

Write *Yes* or *No* to indicate if each sentence is correct.

1. ___ The Minoans invented the sport of soccer.
2. ___ The Minoan Civilization was named after King Minos.
3. ___ The Minoans traded with cities on other Aegean islands.
4. ___ The Minoans were conquered by the Mongols.

The Mycenaeans 1

Fill in the missing vowels from the names of the seas and cities that were in the area of the Minoan and Mycenaean civilizations.

SEAS

1. M __ d __ t __ rr __ n __ __ n
2. Bl __ ck
3. __ __ g __ __ n
4. __ dr __ __ t __ c

CITIES

5. Tr __ y
6. Kn __ ss __ s
7. P __ l __ p __ nn __ s __ s
8. Pyl __ s

The Mycenaeans 2

Fill in the blanks.

walls	fortified
Minoans	invaders
mainland	

Mycenaeans traded with the _____ and adopted much of their culture. One big difference was that their cities were _____ by huge stone _____ to protect them from _____, common on the _____.

The Greek World

The Mycenaeans 3

The Mycenaeans spoke Greek. Identify these Greek words.

1. A brave person:

   H_____

2. A building to worship in:

   C_____

3. A funny play:

   C_____

4. The study of numbers:

   M_____

5. Holds a boat in place:

   A_____

The Mycenaeans 4

Answer on your own paper.

1. What two great epic poems by Homer were about Mycenaean heroes?
2. What war were they about?
3. How long did the war last?
4. What was the Trojan Horse?

The Mycenaeans 5

Why do you think the Mycenaeans attacked the Minoans by invading the island of Crete in 1450 B.C.?

_____

_____

_____

_____

_____

_____

_____

Ancient Greece 1

Greek communities thought of themselves as individual countries even though they all had the same language and heritage. How do you think the geography of Greece contributed to this idea?

_____

_____

_____

_____

_____

_____

The Greek World

Ancient Greece 2

Fill in the blanks.

peninsula	sailors
mountains	traders
farmland	sea

The land of Greece is a

_____. Almost

every part of Greece is near the

_____.

_____ are the major landform in Greece. Only about one-fifth of the land is good as

_____. That is why many Greeks became

_____

and _____.

Ancient Greece 3

The Greeks tried different types of government. Match the types with their definitions.

    a. Oligarchy

    b. Democracy

    c. Aristocracy

____ 1. Government by a ruling class

____ 2. Government by only a few people

____ 3. Government by the people being governed

Ancient Greece 4

List three differences between the way of life in Athens and Sparta.

1. _____

   _____

2. _____

   _____

3. _____

   _____

Ancient Greece 5

Who am I?

_____

Clue one: I was one of the most powerful politicians in Athens.

Clue two: I am known for making Athens a beautiful city.

Clue three: I was from an aristocratic family, but I supported democracy.

The Greek World

Ancient Greece 6

| Sparta |
| polis |
| Dark Ages |
| villages |
| Athens |
| declined |
| agora |

Fill in the blanks.

The middle period of Greek civilization was often referred to as the _____. During this time culture _____. There was little contact among various _____. The people gradually organized into many city-states, each called a _____. Each of these had a marketplace called an _____. The best-known of these city-states were _____ and _____.

Ancient Greece 7

Next to each item, write *A* for Athens or *S* for Sparta.

1. ___ Developed a democracy
2. ___ Valued artists, writers, architects, etc.
3. ___ Had the best army
4. ___ Every man served in assembly
5. ___ Led the Delian League
6. ___ Ruled by two kings and a council
7. ___ War most important
8. ___ Had a simple life
9. ___ Studied medicine
10. ___ Had the best navy
11. ___ No art, music, poets

Ancient Greece 8

Unscramble the names of these subjects the Athenians valued. The first letter of each has been underlined to get you started.

1. P̲ I L H S H Y O O P _____
2. D C I E M̲ N E I _____
3. T E M̲ A C S I T M A H _____
4. C H T U A̲ I T E R E R C _____
5. T A R E U T E R I L̲ _____
6. A R M D̲ A _____
7. N C I C E S̲ E _____
8. T S A̲ R _____
9. C U N O E̲ A T D I _____
10. T O P̲ E Y R _____

The Greek World

Ancient Greece 9

Circle the facts about the Parthenon that are true.

1. It took 20 years to build the Parthenon.
2. The Parthenon was considered the home of the goddess Athena.
3. The Parthenon was made of marble.
4. The Parthenon had rectangular columns.
5. A statue of Athena was inside the Parthenon.

Ancient Greece 10

Write *T* for true or *F* for false.

1. ____ Socrates was one of the most influential figures in history.
2. ____ He is known through the works of his pupil Plato.
3. ____ Socrates lived in Sparta.
4. ____ To him, the most important thing was to "know thyself."
5. ____ Socrates believed individuals should be guided by reason.

Ancient Greece 11

Check the true statements about Spartan boys.

1. ____ Military training began for Spartan boys at age 7.
2. ____ Spartan boys had only one cloak and a thin mat for sleeping on.
3. ____ Spartan boys were given lots of meat to eat.
4. ____ Spartan boys were expected to endure pain and hardship quietly.

Ancient Greece 12

List the three sections a Greek boy's education was divided into and tell what they learned in each section.

1. _____

   _____

2. _____

   _____

3 _____

   _____

The Greek World

Ancient Greece 13

1. What was an acropolis? _____

   _____

   _____

2. What was an agora? _____

   _____

   _____

Ancient Greece 14

Write *T* for true or *F* for false.

1. ___ Slaves did much of the work in Greece.

2. ___ Slaves were mostly other Greeks.

3. ___ Slaves worked in homes, mines, and on farms.

4. ___ Some household slaves were treated like family members.

Ancient Greece 15

Fill in the blanks.

unnoticed	vote
property	home
responsibility	

Women in Athens primarily stayed at _____. They could not own _____ or _____ in elections. Running the home was their primary _____. They were expected to be almost _____ as they did their jobs.

Ancient Greece 16

The Olympic Games originated during the Classical Greek Period as an outgrowth of the athletic training Greek boys received. Name three of the sports they learned.

1. _____

2. _____

3 _____

The Greek World

Ancient Greece 17

In Greek mythology, there was a god or goddess who ruled every aspect of life. Do you know which god or goddess did what?

1. ____ The god of all other gods
2. ____ The god of war
3. ____ The goddess of hunting
4. ____ The god of love
5. ____ The goddess of wisdom
6. ____ The god of the sea
7. ____ The goddess of love and beauty
8. ____ The god of music and poetry
9. ____ The god of science and invention
10. ____ The god of the underworld

a. Apollo	b. Aphrodite
c. Zeus	d. Athena
e. Poseidon	f. Hades
g. Artemis	h. Hermes
i. Eros	j. Ares

Ancient Greece 18

By each famous Greek, write *PH* for philosopher, *PL* for playwright, or *M* for mathematician.

1. _____ Euclid
2. _____ Euripides
3. _____ Socrates
4. _____ Sophocles
5. _____ Plato
6. _____ Aristotle
7. _____ Aristophanes
8. _____ Pythagoras

Aristotle

Ancient Greece 19

Fill in the blanks with the correct letters.

1. The Greeks were the first to form a d _ _ _ _ _ _ _.

2. The Greeks were the first to produce d _ _ _ _ _.

3. The Greeks were the first to write h _ _ _ _ _ _ _.

The Greek World

Ancient Greece 20

Fill in the blanks

chorus	tragedies	dramas
comedies	scenes	disaster

Athenians were the first people to write _____. Some of the

most famous were _____. These plays often ended in

_____. A _____ would come on stage and chant

between _____. Some plays were _____ that

made fun of well-known citizens.

Ancient Greece 21

Fill in the blanks.

Delian
League
expand
Sparta
Athens

Athens attacked smaller city-states to _____

their empire. This upset _____, and they formed

the Peloponnesian _____. In 431, this league declared war on

the _____ League. The Peloponnesian War lasted 27 years.

In the end, _____ was defeated.

Ancient Greece 22

Can you arrange these subjects on the grid below to find out what the one thing the Greeks in Athens valued above many others was?

1.
2.
3.
4.
5.
6.

poetry
paintings
music
buildings
dance
sculptures

The Greek World

Alexander the Great 1

Check the facts about Alexander the Great that are correct.

1. ___ His tutor was Plato.

2. ___ He was a great warrior and scholar.

3. ___ He became king when his father Philip was assassinated.

4. ___ He died at the age of 82.

5. ___ He spread Greek culture to a large portion of the world.

Alexander the Great 2

Fill in the blanks.

| Egypt general revolt restored Persia died |

At age 20, Alexander the Great _____ order to his small empire and suppressed a _____ in Thessaly. He was then chosen to be a _____ of the Greek forces. After reuniting the old city-states of Greece, he decided to attack _____. He was successful and went on from there to invade _____, the Indus Valley, and Iran. He _____ at age 32.

Alexander the Great 3

What am I?

_____

Clue one: I am one of the seven wonders of the ancient world.

Clue two: I was built in Alexandria, Egypt.

Clue three: I was a beacon for sailors for more than 1,500 years.

Alexander the Great 4

Name four modern-day countries that are located in the region of Alexander the Great's empire.

1. _____

2. _____

3 _____

4. _____

The Romans

The Romans 1

Fill in the blanks.

shepherd
Mars
Romulus
wolf
Remus
Tiber

The story of Rome's beginning is told in a legend about twin boys named _____ and _____. They were the sons of the God of War, _____. According to the legend, the twins were abandoned on the banks of the _____ River, were rescued by a _____, and raised by a kind _____. Later, Romulus killed his brother Remus and named the city of Rome after himself.

The Romans 2

Fill in the blanks.

arches   bridges   concrete   open   water   architects

Roman _____ built some of the world's most amazing structures. They used _____ in openings of buildings and for _____ channels and _____. They also invented _____, which made it possible for them to create large, _____ spaces.

The Romans 3

Fill in the blanks.

provinces   force   religions   governor   peace

As their empire grew, Romans divided their lands into _____. Each had a Roman _____ and an army. The Romans did not _____ their ways on conquered peoples. They allowed them to keep their _____ and way of life as long as there was _____.

The Romans

The Romans 4

The first era of Rome's history was the Age of Kings. Check the true things about the Age of Kings.

1. ____ Kings of Rome wore togas with purple borders.

2. ____ Roman kings had total power.

3. ____ Roman kings had to contend with an assembly of nobles.

4. ____ Tarquin was the last king.

The Romans 5

Write the definition of each of these terms.

1. republic _____

_____

_____

2. patricians _____

_____

_____

3. plebeians _____

_____

_____

The Romans 6

Write *T* for true or *F* for false.

1. ____ Roman armies conquered most of the Mediterranean countries.

2. ____ Slaves did much of the work in Rome.

3. ____ The patricians and the plebeians got along well in Rome.

4. ____ Everyone who wanted one had a job in Rome.

The Romans 7

During the Punic Wars, the Phoenicians used a special weapon in battle: the elephant. On your own paper, write why you think that succeeded in frightening the Roman soldiers.

The Romans

The Romans 8

Circle all of the true statements about Julius Caesar.

1. Caesar beat out the Senate to become dictator of Rome.
2. Caesar was an intelligent leader.
3. The title "Caesar" came to mean "emperor."
4. Caesar ruled for 40 years.
5. Caesar was assassinated by members of the Senate.

The Romans 9

One of the greatest Roman buildings was the Colosseum. List three things you know about the building.

1. _____

   _____

2. _____

   _____

3 _____

   _____

The Romans 10

Write the purpose of each of these Roman structures.

1. Aqueducts: _____

   _____

   _____

2. The Pantheon: _____

   _____

   _____

3. The Forum Romanum: _____

   _____

   _____

The Romans 11

Write T for true or F for false.

1. ___ Gladiators were trained in hand-to-hand combat.
2. ___ Gladiators usually fought to the death.
3. ___ All gladiators were slaves and prisoners.
4. ___ The crowds bet on the gladiators.
5. ___ Gladiators sometimes fought animals.

The Romans

The Romans 12

Fill in the vowels of these Roman emperors' and citizens' names.

1. _ _ g _ st _ s
2. C _ l _ g _ l _
3. N _ r _
4. _ ct _ v _ _ n
5. H _ dr _ _ n
6. _ _ r _ l _ _ s

Which of these people were considered good leaders? Why? Answer on your own paper.

The Romans 13

Unscramble these letters to identify the five modern languages that come from Latin.

1. P N H S A I S

_____

2. T G S E P R U E O U

_____

3. N E R F H C

_____

4. R N O A M I N A

_____

5. T L A N I A I

_____

The Romans 14

Match the Latin phrase with the English meaning.

1. ____ post mortem
2. ____ quid pro quo
3. ____ bona fide
4. ____ addendum
5. ____ modus operandi
6. ____ per capita
7. ____ alma mater
8. ____ et cetera

a. authentic, sincere
b. an addition
c. for every person
d. the school you attended
e. and so forth
f. after death
g. method of operating
h. something for something

The Romans

The Romans 15

Match the Roman god or goddess described below with his or her name.

1. ___ god of the sea

2. ___ goddess of love

3. ___ protector of women

4. ___ god of war

5. ___ master of all the gods

6. ___ messenger of the gods

7. ___ goddess of earth, crops, and grains

8. ___ goddess of the moon and hunting

a. Jupiter

b. Venus

c. Diana

d. Juno

e. Neptune

f. Ceres

g. Mercury

h. Mars

The Romans 16

Write the month's name derived from the Latin word below:

1. Mars _____

2. Octo _____

3. Aperire _____

4. Julius _____

5. Septem _____

The Romans 17

Check the things Roman culture has provided us today.

1. ___ The process of making concrete

2. ___ Beautiful works of art

3. ___ The Julian calendar

4. ___ Algebraic methods

5. ___ Knowledge of how to build roads, buildings, bridges, and cities

The Romans

The Romans 18

Fill in the blanks.

persecuted   Constantine
Christians   Augustus
accepted

Jesus Christ was born under the rule of

_____ and died under the rule of Tiberius. Romans kept a

watchful eye on _____. A few emperors tolerated them,

leaving them in peace. Other emperors _____ them. It was not

until _____ converted to Christianity on his deathbed that

the religion was _____ by Romans.

The Romans 19

Circle the true statements about the spread of Christianity.

1. A Jew named Paul traveled the entire region to spread Christianity.

2. Roman officials were not worried about this new religion.

3. The Emperor Nero blamed Christians for Roman problems
   and wanted them killed.

4. Christianity spread despite the torment from the Romans.

The Romans 20

On your own paper, unscramble and rewrite
these sentences about the fall of Rome.

1. among control Romans themselves fought

   for of the government

2. Rome groups weakened Various attacked the European

3. Empire when Visigoths Roman ended The Rome the sacked

Northern Europe

The Celts 1

Match.

1. ____ The lowest class –
   farmers and craftsmen

2. ____ The highest class –
   aristocrats and warriors

3. ____ The middle class –
   priests, teachers,
   judges, and doctors

```
a. Nobles          b. Druids
c. Peasants
```

The Celts 2

Write T for true or F for false.

1. ____ Celts were some of the
   most skillful artisans of their
   time.

2. ____ Celts were master road
   builders.

3. ____ Celts had little to do with art
   and music.

4. ____ Celts had no written
   language.

5. ____ Celts were friendly with the
   Romans.

The Celts 3

Unscramble the names of these current-day countries where the Celts lived.

1. S R A U I A T

   _____

2. H N R Y U G A

   _____

3. K V L S O A I A

   _____

4. M Y N G R E A

   _____

The Celts 4

Fill in the blanks. The first letter is already listed.

The Celts were the first people in Northern Europe to make iron, which they used to make tools. Having iron tools allowed them to clear more l_____, which led to producing more f_____, which led to being able to feed more p_____, which led to looking for more l_____ for those people to live on.

Northern Europe

The Celts 5

Fill in the blanks.

The Celts were the _____

European power around 500 B.C. Instead of

being one nation, their culture was divided into

independent _____.

They were mean and ruthless

_____,

but _____ with those who

were not their _____.

enemies	dominant
friendly	warriors
tribes	

The Vikings 1

The names of most of the days of the week in English are taken from Norse, the Viking language. Identify each day from the Nordic gods and goddesses given.

1. Day of the moon _____

2. Day of Tiu (Norse god of war) _____

3. Day of Thor (Norse god of thunder) _____

4. Day of the sun _____

5. Day of Freya (Norse goddess of love) _____

6. Day of Saturn (a Norse god borrowed from the Romans)

_____

7. Day of Woden or Odin (chief Norse god) _____

Northern Europe

The Vikings 2

Fill in the blanks.

sailors	sagas
farmland	ship
raided	

One reason the Vikings left their homelands was that there was not enough _____.

The Vikings were excellent _____ builders and _____. Some Vikings ruthlessly _____ cities across Europe. Their history was told in stories called _____.

The Vikings 3

What three current-day countries comprise the area in which the Vikings lived?

1. _____

2. _____

3. _____

The Vikings 4

Match these terms with their definitions.

1. ___ Viking homeland
2. ___ Viking assembly of free men
3. ___ A bitter disagreement or fight
4. ___ Memorial stone carved with runic characters

| a. Feud | b. Runestone |
| c. Scandinavia | d. Thing (Althing) |

The Vikings 5

What am I?

_____

Clue one: I am a sea vessel used by the Vikings.

Clue two: I am long and thin with a slight curve at each end.

Clue three: I could sail on seas or sail inland on rivers.

The Western Hemisphere

The Olmecs 1

Unscramble these modern countries' names that make up Mesoamerica.

1. X I E M O C _____

2. Z L E B I E _____

3. D N R S U A O H

   _____

4. T M A L G A E U A

   _____

5. L E D R V L A O A S

   _____

The Olmecs 2

Fill in the blanks.

| Mesoamerica |
| temples |
| corn |
| Mexico |
| pyramids |

The Olmec Civilization developed around 1200 B.C. along the southern coast of

_____. It was one of the first civilizations in

_____.

It began with the discovery of how to grow _____. The Olmecs built _____ and _____ to honor their gods.

The Olmecs 3

Check each of the items below that is an achievement of the Olmecs.

1. ____ Were great sailors

2. ____ Had stone pavements

3. ____ Built drainage systems

4. ____ Made jade sculptures

5. ____ Made the first calendar in the Americas

The Olmecs 4

Unscramble the sentences below and rewrite them correctly on your own paper.

1. huge The stone Olmecs heads carved

2. Stone-Age The had steel Olmecs no tools carve with to

3. transported the without Olmecs heads the wheels of use The

The Western Hemisphere

The Olmecs 5

Identify the features of the Olmec Civilization.

1. Olmecs discovered how to grow this. _____

2. Olmecs worshipped in these structures they built.

    _____

3. Olmecs developed one of the first of these in the Americas.

    _____

4. Olmecs left these, weighing 40 tons and carved from stone.

    _____

The Maya 1

Write *T* for true or *F* for false.

1. ___ The Maya were the most highly developed civilization in Mesoamerica.

2. ___ The Maya lived on the arid coasts of Mexico.

3. ___ Most of the Maya were farmers.

4. ___ The Maya were expert builders.

5. ___ The Maya had no system of writing.

The Maya 2

Identify two differences between the Egyptian pyramids and the Mayan pyramids.

1. _____

    _____

2. _____

    _____

The Maya 3

The Maya developed two calendars.

1. For what did they use their 365-day calendar?

    _____

    _____

2. For what did they use their 260-day calendar?

    _____

    _____

The Western Hemisphere

The Maya 4

How do archaeologists know that the Maya played a game where a ball was driven through a ring? Write your answer on your own paper. Be sure to use complete sentences.

The Maya 5

Fill in the blanks.

> rainwater
> raised
> drain
> methods
> cleared

Mayan farming

_____ allowed them

to thrive. They _____

the rain forest and built fields that

were _____ to

catch and hold _____.

They also built channels to

_____ off excess

water.

The Aztecs 1

Fill in the blanks.

> sign
> prickly
> snake
> wings
> nomadic
> Texcoco
> eagle

The Aztecs were a _____ tribe

that wandered until they were on the borders of Lake

_____. There, they saw an

_____ sitting on the stem of a

_____ pear. The eagle was holding a

_____ in his claws, and his

_____ were open to the sun.

The Aztecs took this as a

_____ from the

gods telling them they should settle there.

The Western Hemisphere

The Aztecs 2

Unscramble the things the people the Aztecs conquered were required to pay tribute with.

1. O F D O _____

2. O C O A C _____

3. W L S E J E _____

4. B R U E B R _____

5. T P O T Y R E

_____

6. T R S H F E E A

_____

The Aztecs 3

Who am I?

_____

Clue one: I am a Spanish conquistador.
Clue two: I conquered the Aztecs.
Clue three: Even though the Aztec emperor Montezuma gave me gold and other valuable gifts, I took him hostage.

The Aztecs 4

Check the things below that the Aztecs had.

1. __ copper   2. __ irrigation

3. __ plows   4. __ bronze

5. __ gold   6. __ terracing

7. __ iron   8. __ calendar

9. __ glass

10. __ mathematics

11. __ steel

12. __ astronomy

The Aztecs 5

Fill in the blanks.

> contend   gunpowder   died
> resist   smallpox   army

Hernando Cortés' _____

had _____, armor,

and horses. This was too much for

the Aztecs to _____

with, but they tried to _____.

Then Tenochtitlán became infected

with _____,

and half of the city _____

The Western Hemisphere

The Incas 1

Fill in the blanks.

> Quechua   Andes   west   Peru   Cuzco   ruler

The Inca civilization developed along the

_____ coast of South America. The

capital city, _____, was in the

_____ Mountains, in modern-day

_____. They spoke the

_____ language. The word "Inca"

in this language means "_____."

The Incas 2

Fill in the blanks.

> stationed   conch   short   relay
> Chasquis   parcel   message

Inca _____ were runners who carried messages

_____-style throughout the Inca kingdom. They were

_____ about every two kilometers along the Incan roads. An

approaching runner would blow his _____ shell to announce

his arrival, and then the waiting Chasqui would receive the

_____ or _____ and carry it to the next

runner. In this manner, news and items traveled far distances in a

_____ period of time.

The Western Hemisphere

The Incas 3

Fill in the vowels of the names of these Incan emperors.

1. P __ ch __ c __ t __

2. H __ __ sc __ r

3. __ t __ h __ __ lp __

4. T __ p __ c

    Y __ p __ nq __ __

The Incas 4

The Incas performed some amazing medical feats. Fill in the blanks to complete each sentence.

1. Incan surgeons performed blood

    _____.

2. Incan surgeons used the jaws

    of _____ to

    clamp wounds closed.

3. Incan surgeons were able

    to perform surgery on the

    _____.

4. They were able to successfully

    _____ limbs.

The Incas 5

What am I?

_____

Clue one: I am a strand of colored strings with knots tied at various places.

Clue two: I probably recorded statistics on population, crops, and weapons.

Clue three: Colors stood for what was being counted and knots stood for how many.

The Incas 6

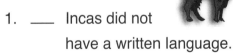
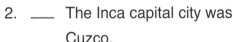

Write *T* for true or *F* for false.

1. ___ Incas did not have a written language.

2. ___ The Inca capital city was Cuzco.

3. ___ Incas used wheeled carts to carry goods.

4. ___ Incas were expert stone masons.

5. ___ Incas rode llamas from city to city.

The Western Hemisphere

The Incas 7

Circle all the words below that are related to the Incas.

suspension bridges   terraces

irrigation canals   wheels

gold treasures   Cortés

Pizarro   llamas

potatoes   Quechua

tunics   horses

The Incas 8

Unscramble these modern countries that exist in what was once the Inca Empire.

1. H L I E C _____

2. D R U E C A O

   _____

3. E P U R _____

4. O L V B I A I

   _____

5. G T N A R E I A N

   _____

The Incas 9

What am I?

_____

Clue one: I was discovered in 1911
             by Hiram Bingham.

Clue two: I sit atop a mountain
             7,000 feet up, so I
             escaped discovery
             and destruction by the
             Spanish.

Clue three: I was probably a royal
             estate founded by
             Pachacuti.

The Incas 10

Match.

a. Sweat of the Sun   b. Coya
c. Sapa Inca   d. Inti
e. Aclla

1. ____ the Inca sun god

2. ____ gold

3. ____ chosen women

4. ____ the chief Inca

5. ____ wife of the Inca chief

Answer Keys

Prehistory 1 (p. 2)
1. archaeologist   2. historian
3. oral traditions   4. prehistory
5. artifacts   6. fossils

Prehistory 2 (p. 2)
Answers will vary. Possibilities include that the type of soil available and access to water determine if a people settle there; isolation from mountains or other natural barriers offer protection from invaders and the influence of outsiders.

Prehistory 3 (p. 3)
1. people who move around and have no settled home
2. soil which contains substances needed for plant growth
3. canals dug to carry water from its source to where it's needed
4. a society with cities, a central government, workers who specialize

Prehistory 4 (p. 3)
1. People used simple stone tools.
2. People were primarily nomads.
3. People lived in caves or camped.
4. Each family or group ruled itself.

Prehistory 5 (p. 3)
1. baskets   2. leather goods
3. tools   4. pottery
5. clothing   6. musical instruments

Fertile Crescent & Mesopotamia 1 (p. 4)
1. Animals and grains were found naturally in abundance and provided a permanent source of food.
2. It was easier to grow crops because of the fertile soil, so there was no need to move around.

Fertile Crescent & Mesopotamia 2 (p. 4)
1. Israel   2. Lebanon
3. Syria   4. Iraq
5. Iran   6. Saudi Arabia

Fertile Crescent & Mesopotamia 3 (p. 4)
1. the Tigris and Euphrates Rivers
2. Turkey, Syria, Iraq (any two)

Fertile Crescent & Mesopotamia 4 (p. 4)
civilization, city-states, language/government, cultures

Fertile Crescent & Mesopotamia 5 (p. 5)
Sentences #1, #3, and #4 should be checked.

The Sumerians 1 (p. 5)
The following should be circled: written language, wheel, water clock, sailboat, plow, twelve-month calendar

The Sumerians 2 (p. 5)
1. T   2. T   3. F   4. T

The Sumerians 3 (p. 5)
This was a disadvantage because attacking armies could easily march into Sumeria from any direction.

The Sumerians 4 (p. 6)
1. pictures carved into clay to represent something
2. professional writers
3. a wedge-shaped instrument for carving on clay tablets
4. a type of writing invented by the Sumerians that replaced pictures with shapes and lines

The Sumerians 5 (p. 6)
Change Greece to Mesopotamia, Nile to Euphrates, flooding to irrigation, pyramids to ziggurats, fifty to sixty, and distance to time.

Babylonia 1 (p. 6)
1. Wall   2. Gate   3. Gardens
4. Gardens   5. Wall   6. Gate

Babylonia 2 (p. 7)
1. Yes   2. No   3. Yes   4. No

Babylonia 3 (p. 7)
1. Protected the weak
2. Carved on a stone column for all to see
3. Eye-for-eye punishments
4. Applied to women and slaves

Babylonia 4 (p. 7)
eclipses, movement, future, planets

Babylonia 5 (p. 7)
Answers will vary.

The Assyrians 1 (p. 8)
1. T   2. T   3. F   4. T

The Assyrians 2 (p. 8)
Standing armies have soldiers who are always in the army. It is their career. A citizen-soldier army has soldiers who fight, and when the war is done, they return to their homes and other careers.

The Assyrians 3 (p. 8)
#2 should be circled. Answers about Assyrian achievements will vary.

The Assyrians 4 (p. 8)
Checks should be placed by the following: chariots, cavalry, archers, foot soldiers, weapons made of iron, iron-tipped battering rams

The Assyrians 5 (p. 9)
fort, governor, king, soldiers, mercenaries

The Hittites 1 (p. 9)
1. Egypt
2. They promised not to fight and to protect each other from attacks.

The Hittites 2 (p. 9)
1. T   2. T   3. F   4. T   5. F

The Hittites 3 (p. 10)
peasants, Anatolia, civilizations, religion, Labarnas, Turkey

The Hittites 4 (p. 10)
1. d   2. b   3. a   4. c

The Hittites 5 (p. 10)
The following phrases should be circled: signed a treaty, developed the process of smelting, were warlike, introduced horses to the Middle East

The Phoenicians 1 (p. 11)
1. F   2. T   3. T   4. T

The Phoenicians 2 (p. 11)
Tyre/Sidon, dye, purple, expensive, royalty

The Phoenicians 3 (p. 11)
1. Cuneiform had pictographs that had pictures representing objects. The Phoenician alphabet had symbols representing sounds.
2. 22
3. A consonant sound

The Phoenicians 4 (p. 11)
1. colored glassware
2. ivory and wood carvings
3. embroidered cloth
4. pottery
5. wine

The Phoenicians 5 (p. 12)
1. change building to sailing
2. change red to purple
3. change Black to Mediterranean
4. change thing to sound

The Hebrews 1 (p. 12)
Monotheism is the belief in one god, and polytheism is the belief in many gods.

The Hebrews 2 (p. 12)
1. Abraham
2. Moses
3. David
4. Saul
5. Solomon

The Hebrews 3 (p. 12)
The Ten Commandments

The Hebrews 4 (p. 13)
Abraham, Canaan, famine, Egypt, enslaved, pharaoh

The Hebrews 5 (p. 13)
(Any order)
Judaism, Christianity, Islam

The Persians 1 (p. 13)
Sentences number #1, #3, and #4 should be checked.

The Persians 2 (p. 14)
1. Avesta
2. Zoroaster
3. Ahura Mazda
4. Ahriman

The Persians 3 (p. 14)
Change Alexander to Darius, 12 to 20, Avestas to Satrapies, sultan to satrap, water to road or highway, and fears to trade.

The Persians 4 (p. 14)

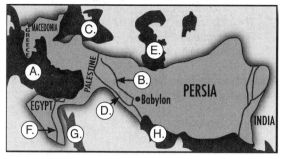

A. The Mediterranean Sea
B. The Tigris River
C. The Black Sea
D. The Euphrates River
E. The Caspian Sea
F. The Nile River
G. The Red Sea
H. The Persian Gulf

Ancient Egypt 1 (p. 15)
Change Amazon to Nile; grass to soil or silt; latest to earliest; 1,000 to 3,000; Yellow to Black; and mountains to deserts.

Ancient Egypt 2 (p. 15)
1. 674   2. 2,143   3. 12,125   4. 327

Ancient Egypt 3 (p. 15)
1. c   2. e   3. a   4. d   5. b

Ancient Egypt 4 (p. 16)
1. Sphinx
2. pyramids
3. canals
4. temples

Ancient Egypt 5 (p. 16)
1. papyrus
2. pharaoh
3. pyramid
4. mummies
5. hieroglyphics

Ancient Egypt 6 (p. 16)
gold, slaves, and ivory

Ancient Egypt 7 (p. 16)
1. c   2. a   3. b   4. c
5. b   6. a   7. c   8. a

Ancient Egypt 8 (p. 17)
The following words should be circled: pyramids, Nile, hieroglyphics, pharaoh, nomarchs, Khufu, papyrus, scribes, Aton, mummies, Thebes

Ancient Egypt 9 (p. 17)
Sentences #2, #3, and #4 should be checked.

Ancient Egypt 10 (p. 17)
The desert and seas that surround Egypt on all sides kept invaders out for the most part.

Ancient Egypt 11 (p. 17)
1. T   2. T   3. F   4. T

Ancient Egypt 12 (p. 18)
1. F   2. T   3. T   4. F   5. T

Ancient Egypt 13 (p. 18)
The following should be circled: They had absolute power.; They were believed to be gods.; They owned all land and water.; They were religious leaders.

Ancient Egypt 14 (p. 18)
a. 3   b. 4   c. 1   d. 5
e. 2

Ancient Egypt 15 (p. 18)
Nubia, Bow, tradesmen, gold

Ancient Egypt 16 (p. 19)
The Rosetta Stone had the same message carved in three different languages: hieroglyphics, Egyptian demotic, and Greek. Champollion was the first to decode the hieroglyphics in 1822. This made it possible to read other Egyptian hieroglyphics.

Ancient Egypt 17 (p. 19)
1. No   2. Yes   3. Yes   4. Yes
5. Yes

Ancient Egypt 18 (p. 19)
1. They had many different occupations.
2. They could own property.
3. Some were in charge of temples.
4. They worked in the fields with men.

Indus Valley 1 (p. 20)
The following phrases should be circled:
undeciphered language,
larger cities than Sumeria,
drainage and sewer system,
uncovered in 1921,
well-planned cities,
grew cotton

Indus Valley 2 (p. 20)
Answers will vary.

Indus Valley 3 (p. 20)
1. barley   2. wheat   3. dates
4. cattle   5. chickens   6. buffalo

Indus Valley 4 (p. 20)
    Many civilizations sprang up along the banks of large rivers because the rivers provided water for growing crops, washing, and drinking. Sometimes the rivers overflowed and left valuable nutrients in the soil.

Indus Valley 5 (p. 21)
Pakistan, Indus, Ganges, Harappa/Mohenjo-daro, cotton

Ancient India 1 (p. 21)
Alexander, Babylon, thousand, artists, ideas, Sanskrit

Ancient India 2 (p. 21)
1. Yes   2. Yes   3. Yes   4. No
5. Yes/No (Either is acceptable; the Chinese may have discovered it during the same time.)

Ancient India 3 (p. 22)
beliefs, many, spirit, gods/goddesses

Ancient India 4 (p. 22)
1. How you lived your life
2. You might come back as an animal or a member of a lower caste.
3. You would be freed from the cycle of rebirth.

Ancient India 5 (p. 22)
1. Yes   2. Yes   3. No   4. Yes
5. Yes

Ancient China 1 (p. 23)
1. T   2. T   3. T   4. F

Ancient China 2 (p. 23)
muddiest, Yellow, soil, plains, farming

Ancient China 3 (p. 23)
    The Huang He River flooded unpredictably, killing many people and destroying homes and crops.

Ancient China 4 (p. 23)
1. The Shang people built the first cities in China.
2. The Shang people were some of the finest bronze workers in China.
3. The Shang people invented China's first writing.

Ancient China 5 (p. 24)
1. Many generations lived together.
2. The oldest male had top authority.
3. Parents chose spouses.
4. Chinese family names are first.

Ancient China 6 (p. 24)
united, Qin, dynasty, harsh, Great Wall

Ancient China 7 (p. 24)
Han, stable, Antioch, Silk, ideas

Ancient China 8 (p. 25)
Confucius

Ancient China 9 (p. 25)
Circle the following words: silk, rockets, chess, book printing, kites, gunpowder, fireworks, paper, wheelbarrows, matches, abacus, porcelain

Ancient China 10 (p. 25)
1. L   2. C   3. C   4. L   5. C

Ancient China 11 (p. 25)
Silk worm

Ancient China 12 (p. 26)
Answers will vary.

Ancient China 13 (p. 26)
Sentences #2, #3, and #5 should be circled.

Ancient China 14 (p. 26)
    The stability of the Han dynasty allowed them the time and the economic means to focus on other things instead of fighting.

Ancient China 15 (p. 27)
1. Shang   2. Chou   3. Manchu
4. Ming   5. Tang   6. Sui
7. Qin   8. Zhou   9. Han
10. Xia   11. Song

The Mongols 1 (p. 27)
Genghis Khan

The Mongols 2 (p. 27)
largest, feared, animals, brutal, destroyed, Asia, Europe

The Mongols 3 (p. 28)
Sentences #1, #2, and #4 should be checked.

The Mongols 4 (p. 28)
1. soldier
2. barbarians
3. horses
4. weapons

The Mongols 5 (p. 28)
revolted, Ming, ruled, erase, Beijing

The Minoans 1 (p. 29)
1. T   2. T   3. F   4. T   5. T

The Minoans 2 (p. 29)
sports, boxing/bull-jumping, horns, somersault, feet

The Minoans 3 (p. 29)
1. All Minoans had comfortable homes.
2. Most Minoan homes were two stories.
3. Many Minoans were craftsmen.
4. Each Minoan town had a palace.

The Minoans 4 (p. 30)
Being on an island meant they were isolated and didn't have to worry about attacks as much as other societies on the mainland. They could spend their resources on economic development rather than defense.

The Minoans 5 (p. 30)
1. No   2. Yes   3. Yes   4. No

The Mycenaeans 1 (p. 30)
1. Mediterranean   2. Black   3. Aegean
4. Adriatic   5. Troy   6. Knossus
7. Peloponnesus or Peloponnisos 8. Pylos

The Mycenaeans 2 (p. 30)
Minoans, fortified, walls, invaders, mainland

The Mycenaeans 3 (p. 31)
1. Hero
2. Church
3. Comedy
4. Mathematics
5. Anchor

The Mycenaeans 4 (p. 31)
1. *Illiad, Odyssey*
2. The wars between the Greeks and Troy (Trojan War)
3. Ten years
4. Greek soldiers hid inside a giant wooden horse. The Trojans took it into their city. At night, the soldiers came out and attacked Troy.

The Mycenaeans 5 (p. 31)
Answers will vary. One possibility is they were jealous of the wealth and lifestyle the Minoans had.

Ancient Greece 1 (p. 31)
Being many islands and peninsulas with mountains, it was difficult for people to get from one area to another, so they didn't mix much.

Ancient Greece 2 (p. 32)
peninsula, sea, Mountains, farmland, traders/sailors

Ancient Greece 3 (p. 32)
1. c   2. a   3. b

Ancient Greece 4 (p. 32)
Answers will vary.

Ancient Greece 5 (p. 32)
Pericles

Ancient Greece 6 (p. 33)
Dark Ages, declined, villages, polis, agora, Athens/Sparta

Ancient Greece 7 (p. 33)
1. A   2. A   3. S   4. A   5. A   6. S
7. S   8. S   9. A   10. A   11. S

Ancient Greece 8 (p. 33)
1. philosophy   2. medicine
3. mathematics   4. architecture
5. literature   6. drama
7. science   8. arts
9. education   10. poetry

Ancient Greece 9 (p. 34)
Sentences #2, #3, and #5 should be circled.

Ancient Greece 10 (p. 34)
1. T   2. T   3. F   4. T   5. T

Ancient Greece 11 (p. 34)
Sentences #1, #2, and #4 should be checked.

Ancient Greece 12 (p. 34)
1. letters: reading, writing, and math
2. music: to play an instrument and sing
3. athletics: wrestling, jumping, running, gymnastics, discus or javelin

Ancient Greece 13 (p. 35)
1. A high, rocky hill where the Greeks built cities
2. A public market or meeting place in Greek cities

Ancient Greece 14 (p. 35)
1. T   2. F   3. T   4. T

Ancient Greece 15 (p. 35)
home, property, vote, responsibility, unnoticed

Ancient Greece 16 (p. 35)
wrestling, running, jumping, gymnastics, discus, and javelin throwing (any three)

Ancient Greece 17 (p. 36)
1. c   2. j   3. g   4. i   5. d
6. e   7. b   8. a   9. h   10. f

Ancient Greece 18 (p. 36)
1. M   2. PL   3. PH   4. PL
5. PH   6. PH   7. PL   8. M

Ancient Greece 19 (p. 36)
1. democracy   2. dramas   3. histories

Ancient Greece 20 (p. 37)
dramas, tragedies, disaster, chorus, scenes, comedies

Ancient Greece 21 (p. 37)
expand, Sparta, League, Delian, Athens

Ancient Greece 22 (p. 37)
1. buildings   2. dance   3. paintings
4. music   5. sculptures   6. poetry
The word down the middle column is *beauty.*

Alexander the Great 1 (p. 38)
Sentences #2, #3, and #5 should be checked.

Alexander the Great 2 (p. 38)
restored, revolt, general, Persia, Egypt, died

Alexander the Great 3 (p. 38)
The Lighthouse of Alexandria (on the island of Pharos)

Alexander the Great 4 (p. 38)
Any four of these: Macedonia, Greece, Turkey, Bulgaria, Iran, Iraq, Lebanon, Syria, Egypt, Pakistan, Afghanistan, Jordan, Israel, Turkmenistan, Tajikistan, Uzbekistan, Kyrgyzstan

The Romans 1 (p. 39)
Romulus/Remus, Mars, Tiber, wolf, shepherd

The Romans 2 (p. 39)
architects, arches, water, bridges, concrete, open

The Romans 3 (p. 39)
provinces, governor, force, religions, peace

The Romans 4 (p. 40)
Sentences #1, #3, and #4 should be checked.

The Romans 5 (p. 40)
1. A republic is a form of government where citizens who have the right to vote elect leaders.
2. The patricians were the upper class, rich citizens of Rome. They owned land, had slaves, etc.
3. The plebeians were the ordinary citizens of Rome: the shopkeepers and craftsmen.

The Romans 6 (p. 40)
1. T   2. T   3. F   4. F

The Romans 7 (p. 40)
The Romans had not seen elephants and were frightened by their sheer size and their ability to easily smash through enemy lines.

The Romans 8 (p. 41)
Sentences #1, #2, #3, and #5 should be circled.

The Romans 9 (p. 41)
Answers will vary.

The Romans 10 (p. 41)
1. To carry water into the city from the springs
2. To worship in (like a temple)
3. A public square; a favorite place for making speeches

The Romans 11 (p. 41)
1. T   2. T   3. F   4. T   5. T

The Romans 12 (p. 42)
1. Augustus   2. Caligula
3. Nero   4. Octavian
5. Hadrian   6. Aurelius
Augustus, who was also called Octavian; Hadrian; and Aurelius were all good leaders. Nero and Caligula were both bad (and probably insane).

The Romans 13 (p. 42)
1. Spanish   2. Portuguese   3. French
4. Romanian   5. Italian

The Romans 14 (p. 42)
1. f   2. h   3. a   4. b
5. g   6. c   7. d   8. e

The Romans 15 (p. 43)
1. e   2. b   3. d   4. h
5. a   6. g   7. f   8. c

The Romans 16 (p. 43)
1. March   2. October   3. April
4. July   5. September

The Romans 17 (p. 43)
Items #1, #2, #3, and #5 should be checked.

The Romans 18 (p. 44)
Augustus, Christians, persecuted, Constantine, accepted

The Romans 19 (p. 44)
Sentences #1, #3, and #4 should be circled.

The Romans 20 (p. 44)
1. Romans fought among themselves for control of the government.
2. Various European groups attacked the weakened Rome.
3. The Roman Empire ended when the Visigoths sacked Rome.

The Celts 1 (p. 45)
1. c   2. a   3. b

The Celts 2 (p. 45)
1. T   2. T   3. F   4. T   5. F

The Celts 3 (p. 45)
1. Austria   2. Hungary
3. Slovakia   4. Germany

The Celts 4 (p. 45)
land, food, people, land

The Celts 5 (p. 46)
dominant, tribes, warriors, friendly, enemies

The Vikings 1 (p. 46)
1. Monday   2. Tuesday   3. Thursday
4. Sunday   5. Friday   6. Saturday
7. Wednesday

The Vikings 2 (p. 47)
farmland, ship, sailors, raided, sagas

The Vikings 3 (p. 47)
Norway, Sweden, and Denmark

The Vikings 4 (p. 47)
1. c   2. d   3. a   4. b

The Vikings 5 (p. 47)
A Viking longship

The Olmecs 1 (p. 48)
1. Mexico   2. Belize   3. Honduras
4. Guatemala   5. El Salvador

The Olmecs 2 (p. 48)
Mexico, Mesoamerica, corn, temples/pyramids

The Olmecs 3 (p. 48)
Items #2, #3, #4, and #5 should be checked.

The Olmecs 4 (p. 48)
1. The Olmecs carved huge stone heads.
2. The Stone-Age Olmecs had no steel tools to carve with.
3. The Olmecs transported the heads without the use of wheels.

The Olmecs 5 (p. 49)
1. corn   2. temples or pyramids
3. calendars   4. heads

The Maya 1 (p. 49)
1. T   2. F   3. T   4. T   5. F

The Maya 2 (p. 49)
Answers will vary. Some possibilities: Egyptian pyramids were tombs for dead kings, while Mayan pyramids were religious ceremonial sites. Mayan pyramids had steps up the sides and usually some kind of temple on top.

The Maya 3 (p. 49)
1. To plant and harvest crops
2. To mark religious ceremonies

The Maya 4 (p. 50)
They found ball courts in every large city of the Maya. These courts are similar to those found in other ancient cultures in the Americas.

The Maya 5 (p. 50)
methods, cleared, raised, rainwater, drain

The Aztecs 1 (p. 50)
nomadic, Texcoco, eagle, prickly, snake, wings, sign

The Aztecs 2 (p. 51)
1. food   2. cocoa   3. jewels
4. rubber   5. pottery   6. feathers

The Aztecs 3 (p. 51)
Hernando Cortés

The Aztecs 4 (p. 51)
Checks should be placed by the following items:

1. copper	2. irrigation
4. bronze	5. gold
6. terracing	8. calendar
10. mathematics	12. astronomy

The Aztecs 5 (p. 51)
army, gunpowder, contend, resist, smallpox, died

The Incas 1 (p. 52)
west, Cuzco, Andes, Peru, Quechua, ruler

The Incas 2 (p. 52)
Chasquis, relay, stationed, conch, message/parcel, short

The Incas 3 (p. 53)
1. Pachacuti
2. Huascar
3. Atahualpa
4. Topac Yupanqui

The Incas 4 (p. 53)

1. transfusions	2. ants
3. brain	4. amputate

The Incas 5 (p. 53)
A quipu

The Incas 6 (p. 53)
1. T   2. T   3. F   4. T   5. F

The Incas 7 (p. 54)
The following words should be circled: suspension bridges, terraces, irrigation canals, gold treasures, Pizarro, llamas, potatoes, Quechua, tunics

The Incas 8 (p. 54)

1. Chile	2. Ecuador
3. Peru	4. Bolivia
5. Argentina	

The Incas 9 (p. 54)
City of Machu Picchu

The Incas 10 (p. 54)
1. d   2. a   3. e   4. c   5. b